Password Book

A

Website _____

Username _____

Password _____

Notes _____

Website _____

Username _____

Password _____

Notes _____

Website _____

Username _____

Password _____

Notes _____

Website _____

Username _____

Password _____

Notes _____

Website

Username

Password

Notes

Website

Username

Password

Notes

Website

Username

Password

Notes

Website

Username

Password

Notes

A

Website

Username

Password

Notes

Website

Username

Password

Notes

Website

Username

Password

Notes

Website

Username

Password

Notes

Website

Username

Password

Notes

Website

Username

Password

Notes

Website

Username

Password

Notes

Website

Username

Password

Notes

B

Website _____

Username _____

Password _____

Notes _____

Website _____

Username _____

Password _____

Notes _____

Website _____

Username _____

Password _____

Notes _____

Website _____

Username _____

Password _____

Notes _____

Website

Username

Password

Notes

Website

Username

Password

Notes

Website

Username

Password

Notes

Website

Username

Password

Notes

B

Website _____

Username _____

Password _____

Notes _____

Website _____

Username _____

Password _____

Notes _____

Website _____

Username _____

Password _____

Notes _____

Website _____

Username _____

Password _____

Notes _____

Website

Username

Password

Notes

Website

Username

Password

Notes

Website

Username

Password

Notes

Website

Username

Password

Notes

C

Website _____

Username _____

Password _____

Notes _____

Website _____

Username _____

Password _____

Notes _____

Website _____

Username _____

Password _____

Notes _____

Website _____

Username _____

Password _____

Notes _____

Website

Username

Password

Notes

Website

Username

Password

Notes

Website

Username

Password

Notes

Website

Username

Password

Notes

C

Website _____

Username _____

Password _____

Notes _____

Website _____

Username _____

Password _____

Notes _____

Website _____

Username _____

Password _____

Notes _____

Website _____

Username _____

Password _____

Notes _____

Website _____

Username _____

Password _____

Notes _____

Website _____

Username _____

Password _____

Notes _____

Website _____

Username _____

Password _____

Notes _____

Website _____

Username _____

Password _____

Notes _____

D

Website _____

Username _____

Password _____

Notes _____

Website _____

Username _____

Password _____

Notes _____

Website _____

Username _____

Password _____

Notes _____

Website _____

Username _____

Password _____

Notes _____

Website

Username

Password

Notes

Website

Username

Password

Notes

Website

Username

Password

Notes

Website

Username

Password

Notes

D

Website

Username

Password

Notes

Website

Username

Password

Notes

Website

Username

Password

Notes

Website

Username

Password

Notes

Website

Username

Password

Notes

Website

Username

Password

Notes

Website

Username

Password

Notes

Website

Username

Password

Notes

E

Website _____

Username _____

Password _____

Notes _____

Website _____

Username _____

Password _____

Notes _____

Website _____

Username _____

Password _____

Notes _____

Website _____

Username _____

Password _____

Notes _____

Website

Username

Password

Notes

Website

Username

Password

Notes

Website

Username

Password

Notes

Website

Username

Password

Notes

E

Website _____

Username _____

Password _____

Notes _____

Website _____

Username _____

Password _____

Notes _____

Website _____

Username _____

Password _____

Notes _____

Website _____

Username _____

Password _____

Notes _____

Website

Username

Password

Notes

Website

Username

Password

Notes

Website

Username

Password

Notes

Website

Username

Password

Notes

F

Website

Username

Password

Notes

Website

Username

Password

Notes

Website

Username

Password

Notes

Website

Username

Password

Notes

Website

Username

Password

Notes

Website

Username

Password

Notes

Website

Username

Password

Notes

Website

Username

Password

Notes

F

Website _____

Username _____

Password _____

Notes _____

Website _____

Username _____

Password _____

Notes _____

Website _____

Username _____

Password _____

Notes _____

Website _____

Username _____

Password _____

Notes _____

Website

Username

Password

Notes

Website

Username

Password

Notes

Website

Username

Password

Notes

Website

Username

Password

Notes

G

Website

Username

Password

Notes

Website

Username

Password

Notes

Website

Username

Password

Notes

Website

Username

Password

Notes

Website

Username

Password

Notes

Website

Username

Password

Notes

Website

Username

Password

Notes

Website

Username

Password

Notes

G

Website _____

Username _____

Password _____

Notes _____

Website _____

Username _____

Password _____

Notes _____

Website _____

Username _____

Password _____

Notes _____

Website _____

Username _____

Password _____

Notes _____

Website

Username

Password

Notes

Website

Username

Password

Notes

Website

Username

Password

Notes

Website

Username

Password

Notes

H

Website _____

Username _____

Password _____

Notes _____

Website _____

Username _____

Password _____

Notes _____

Website _____

Username _____

Password _____

Notes _____

Website _____

Username _____

Password _____

Notes _____

Website

Username

Password

Notes

Website

Username

Password

Notes

Website

Username

Password

Notes

Website

Username

Password

Notes

H

Website _____

Username _____

Password _____

Notes _____

Website _____

Username _____

Password _____

Notes _____

Website _____

Username _____

Password _____

Notes _____

Website _____

Username _____

Password _____

Notes _____

Website

Username

Password

Notes

Website

Username

Password

Notes

Website

Username

Password

Notes

Website

Username

Password

Notes

I

Website

Username

Password

Notes

Website

Username

Password

Notes

Website

Username

Password

Notes

Website

Username

Password

Notes

Website

Username

Password

Notes

Website

Username

Password

Notes

Website

Username

Password

Notes

Website

Username

Password

Notes

I

Website _____

Username _____

Password _____

Notes _____

Website _____

Username _____

Password _____

Notes _____

Website _____

Username _____

Password _____

Notes _____

Website _____

Username _____

Password _____

Notes _____

Website _____

Username _____

Password _____

Notes _____

Website _____

Username _____

Password _____

Notes _____

Website _____

Username _____

Password _____

Notes _____

Website _____

Username _____

Password _____

Notes _____

J

Website

Username

Password

Notes

Website

Username

Password

Notes

Website

Username

Password

Notes

Website

Username

Password

Notes

J

Website

Username

Password

Notes

Website

Username

Password

Notes

Website

Username

Password

Notes

Website

Username

Password

Notes

J

Website

Username

Password

Notes

Website

Username

Password

Notes

Website

Username

Password

Notes

Website

Username

Password

Notes

Website

Username

Password

Notes

Website

Username

Password

Notes

Website

Username

Password

Notes

Website

Username

Password

Notes

K

Website

Username

Password

Notes

Website

Username

Password

Notes

Website

Username

Password

Notes

Website

Username

Password

Notes

Website

Username

Password

Notes

Website

Username

Password

Notes

Website

Username

Password

Notes

Website

Username

Password

Notes

K

Website

Username

Password

Notes

Website

Username

Password

Notes

Website

Username

Password

Notes

Website

Username

Password

Notes

Website

Username

Password

Notes

Website

Username

Password

Notes

Website

Username

Password

Notes

Website

Username

Password

Notes

L

Website

Username

Password

Notes

Website

Username

Password

Notes

Website

Username

Password

Notes

Website

Username

Password

Notes

Website

Username

Password

Notes

Website

Username

Password

Notes

Website

Username

Password

Notes

Website

Username

Password

Notes

L

Website _____

Username _____

Password _____

Notes _____

Website _____

Username _____

Password _____

Notes _____

Website _____

Username _____

Password _____

Notes _____

Website _____

Username _____

Password _____

Notes _____

Website

Username

Password

Notes

Website

Username

Password

Notes

Website

Username

Password

Notes

Website

Username

Password

Notes

M

Website _____

Username _____

Password _____

Notes _____

Website _____

Username _____

Password _____

Notes _____

Website _____

Username _____

Password _____

Notes _____

Website _____

Username _____

Password _____

Notes _____

Website

Username

Password

Notes

Website

Username

Password

Notes

Website

Username

Password

Notes

Website

Username

Password

Notes

M

Website

Username

Password

Notes

Website

Username

Password

Notes

Website

Username

Password

Notes

Website

Username

Password

Notes

Website

Username

Password

Notes

Website

Username

Password

Notes

Website

Username

Password

Notes

Website

Username

Password

Notes

N

Website

Username

Password

Notes

Website

Username

Password

Notes

Website

Username

Password

Notes

Website

Username

Password

Notes

Website

Username

Password

Notes

Website

Username

Password

Notes

Website

Username

Password

Notes

Website

Username

Password

Notes

N

Website

Username

Password

Notes

Website

Username

Password

Notes

Website

Username

Password

Notes

Website

Username

Password

Notes

Website _____

Username _____

Password _____

Notes _____

Website _____

Username _____

Password _____

Notes _____

Website _____

Username _____

Password _____

Notes _____

Website _____

Username _____

Password _____

Notes _____

O

Website _____

Username _____

Password _____

Notes _____

Website _____

Username _____

Password _____

Notes _____

Website _____

Username _____

Password _____

Notes _____

Website _____

Username _____

Password _____

Notes _____

O

Website

Username

Password

Notes

Website

Username

Password

Notes

Website

Username

Password

Notes

Website

Username

Password

Notes

O

Website

Username

Password

Notes

Website

Username

Password

Notes

Website

Username

Password

Notes

Website

Username

Password

Notes

O

Website

Username

Password

Notes

Website

Username

Password

Notes

Website

Username

Password

Notes

Website

Username

Password

Notes

P

Website _____

Username _____

Password _____

Notes _____

Website _____

Username _____

Password _____

Notes _____

Website _____

Username _____

Password _____

Notes _____

Website _____

Username _____

Password _____

Notes _____

P

Website

Username

Password

Notes

Website

Username

Password

Notes

Website

Username

Password

Notes

Website

Username

Password

Notes

P

Website _____

Username _____

Password _____

Notes _____

Website _____

Username _____

Password _____

Notes _____

Website _____

Username _____

Password _____

Notes _____

Website _____

Username _____

Password _____

Notes _____

Website

Username

Password

Notes

Website

Username

Password

Notes

Website

Username

Password

Notes

Website

Username

Password

Notes

Q

Website

Username

Password

Notes

Website

Username

Password

Notes

Website

Username

Password

Notes

Website

Username

Password

Notes

Website

Username

Password

Notes

Website

Username

Password

Notes

Website

Username

Password

Notes

Website

Username

Password

Notes

Q

Website

Username

Password

Notes

Website

Username

Password

Notes

Website

Username

Password

Notes

Website

Username

Password

Notes

Website

Username

Password

Notes

Website

Username

Password

Notes

Website

Username

Password

Notes

Website

Username

Password

Notes

R

Website

Username

Password

Notes

Website

Username

Password

Notes

Website

Username

Password

Notes

Website

Username

Password

Notes

Website

Username

Password

Notes

Website

Username

Password

Notes

Website

Username

Password

Notes

Website

Username

Password

Notes

R

Website

Username

Password

Notes

Website

Username

Password

Notes

Website

Username

Password

Notes

Website

Username

Password

Notes

Website

Username

Password

Notes

Website

Username

Password

Notes

Website

Username

Password

Notes

Website

Username

Password

Notes

S

Website

Username

Password

Notes

Website

Username

Password

Notes

Website

Username

Password

Notes

Website

Username

Password

Notes

Website

Username

Password

Notes

Website

Username

Password

Notes

Website

Username

Password

Notes

Website

Username

Password

Notes

S

Website _____

Username _____

Password _____

Notes _____

Website _____

Username _____

Password _____

Notes _____

Website _____

Username _____

Password _____

Notes _____

Website _____

Username _____

Password _____

Notes _____

Website _____

Username _____

Password _____

Notes _____

Website _____

Username _____

Password _____

Notes _____

Website _____

Username _____

Password _____

Notes _____

Website _____

Username _____

Password _____

Notes _____

T

Website

Username

Password

Notes

Website

Username

Password

Notes

Website

Username

Password

Notes

Website

Username

Password

Notes

Website

Username

Password

Notes

Website

Username

Password

Notes

Website

Username

Password

Notes

Website

Username

Password

Notes

T

Website

Username

Password

Notes

Website

Username

Password

Notes

Website

Username

Password

Notes

Website

Username

Password

Notes

Website

Username

Password

Notes

Website

Username

Password

Notes

Website

Username

Password

Notes

Website

Username

Password

Notes

U

Website _____

Username _____

Password _____

Notes _____

Website _____

Username _____

Password _____

Notes _____

Website _____

Username _____

Password _____

Notes _____

Website _____

Username _____

Password _____

Notes _____

Website

Username

Password

Notes

Website

Username

Password

Notes

Website

Username

Password

Notes

Website

Username

Password

Notes

U

Website _____

Username _____

Password _____

Notes _____

Website _____

Username _____

Password _____

Notes _____

Website _____

Username _____

Password _____

Notes _____

Website _____

Username _____

Password _____

Notes _____

Website

Username

Password

Notes

Website

Username

Password

Notes

Website

Username

Password

Notes

Website

Username

Password

Notes

V

Website

Username

Password

Notes

Website

Username

Password

Notes

Website

Username

Password

Notes

Website

Username

Password

Notes

Website

Username

Password

Notes

Website

Username

Password

Notes

Website

Username

Password

Notes

Website

Username

Password

Notes

V

Website

Username

Password

Notes

Website

Username

Password

Notes

Website

Username

Password

Notes

Website

Username

Password

Notes

Website

Username

Password

Notes

Website

Username

Password

Notes

Website

Username

Password

Notes

Website

Username

Password

Notes

W

Website _____

Username _____

Password _____

Notes _____

Website _____

Username _____

Password _____

Notes _____

Website _____

Username _____

Password _____

Notes _____

Website _____

Username _____

Password _____

Notes _____

Website _____

Username _____

Password _____

Notes _____

Website _____

Username _____

Password _____

Notes _____

Website _____

Username _____

Password _____

Notes _____

Website _____

Username _____

Password _____

Notes _____

W

Website _____

Username _____

Password _____

Notes _____

Website _____

Username _____

Password _____

Notes _____

Website _____

Username _____

Password _____

Notes _____

Website _____

Username _____

Password _____

Notes _____

Website _____

Username _____

Password _____

Notes _____

Website _____

Username _____

Password _____

Notes _____

Website _____

Username _____

Password _____

Notes _____

Website _____

Username _____

Password _____

Notes _____

X

Website

Username

Password

Notes

Website

Username

Password

Notes

Website

Username

Password

Notes

Website

Username

Password

Notes

Website _____

Username _____

Password _____

Notes _____

Website _____

Username _____

Password _____

Notes _____

Website _____

Username _____

Password _____

Notes _____

Website _____

Username _____

Password _____

Notes _____

X

Website _____

Username _____

Password _____

Notes _____

Website _____

Username _____

Password _____

Notes _____

Website _____

Username _____

Password _____

Notes _____

Website _____

Username _____

Password _____

Notes _____

Website

Username

Password

Notes

Website

Username

Password

Notes

Website

Username

Password

Notes

Website

Username

Password

Notes

Y

Website

Username

Password

Notes

Website

Username

Password

Notes

Website

Username

Password

Notes

Website

Username

Password

Notes

Website

Username

Password

Notes

Website

Username

Password

Notes

Website

Username

Password

Notes

Website

Username

Password

Notes

Y

Website _____

Username _____

Password _____

Notes _____

Website _____

Username _____

Password _____

Notes _____

Website _____

Username _____

Password _____

Notes _____

Website _____

Username _____

Password _____

Notes _____

Website

Username

Password

Notes

Website

Username

Password

Notes

Website

Username

Password

Notes

Website

Username

Password

Notes

Z

Website _____

Username _____

Password _____

Notes _____

Website _____

Username _____

Password _____

Notes _____

Website _____

Username _____

Password _____

Notes _____

Website _____

Username _____

Password _____

Notes _____

Z

Website _____

Username _____

Password _____

Notes _____

Website _____

Username _____

Password _____

Notes _____

Website _____

Username _____

Password _____

Notes _____

Website _____

Username _____

Password _____

Notes _____

Z

Website _____

Username _____

Password _____

Notes _____

Website _____

Username _____

Password _____

Notes _____

Website _____

Username _____

Password _____

Notes _____

Website _____

Username _____

Password _____

Notes _____

Z

Website _____

Username _____

Password _____

Notes _____

Website _____

Username _____

Password _____

Notes _____

Website _____

Username _____

Password _____

Notes _____

Website _____

Username _____

Password _____

Notes _____

Made in the USA
Lexington, KY
04 December 2018